Spotter's Guide

KT-379-817

TOWN & CITY WILDLIFE

Diana Shipp

Special Consultant
Richard Findon
of the Nature Conservancy Council

Contents

Editorial Director
Sue Jacquemier

Designers
David Bennett, Anne Sharples

Illustrators
Denise Finney, Dee Morgan,
Andy Martin, Ian Jackson,
Julie Piper. A number of the illustrations in
this book have been previously published
in the Usborne *Spotter's Guide* series,
and the *Usborne Guides* series.

Consultants and contributors
Dr June Chatfield, Dr Richard Lane, Pearl
Small, Peter Smith, Alan Stubbs, Dr
Matthew M. Vriends

First published in 1981 by
Usborne Publishing Limited,
20 Garrick Street, London WC2E 9BJ

© 1981 by Usborne Publishing Limited

Printed in Spain by Gráficas Estella, S.A.
Estella (Navarra)

How to use this book

This book is an identification guide to some of the plants and animals that live in towns and cities in Britain and other European countries.

The book is divided into sections dealing with flowers, trees, mosses, fungi, lichens, ferns, grasses, birds, mammals, insects and other invertebrates (animals without backbones).

The description beside each illustration tells you where the species grows or lives, or other things to help you identify it. There is a small circle beside each description. Whenever you see anything new put a tick in the appropriate circle.

The last line of the wild flower captions tells you the months when you usually see each plant in flower. The rest of the plant can often be seen at other times of the year.

There are many kinds of fungi, some of which are deadly poisonous. **Never taste or eat** any fungus unless an expert has helped you identify it.

Capsule

The mosses in this book have been illustrated with their fruiting capsules which contain their spores.

With some birds and insects, the male (♂) and female (♀) are very different. In this case, both sexes are illustrated.

The illustrations of grasses are in black and white. Colours of the grasses are given around each picture. Close-ups of parts of the flowering heads are shown.

The insects and other invertebrates in this book are not drawn to scale. A line beside each picture shows the actual size of the animal.

Scorecard
At the back of the book is a scorecard which gives you a score for each plant or animal you see. A very common species scores 5 and a very rare one is worth 25. You can add up your score after a day's spotting.

Scientific names
Some plants and animals have no common English name — only a scientific Latin name. The first word of the scientific name is the group to which the plant or animal belongs. The second word is the name of the species.

Measuring plants and animals

The drawings on this page show you how plants and animals are measured. The measurements are usually average sizes, given in centimetres (cm), metres (m) or millimetres (mm) in the captions next to the illustrations. The plants and animals in this book are not drawn to scale, so their sizes will help you to identify the different species.

Fungi. Width of cap, given in millimetres or centimetres.

Snail. Width of shell, given in millimetres.

Butterflies, moths and **bats**. Wing span, given in millimetres or centimetres.

Other insects. Body length, excluding antennae, given in millimetres.

Spiders. Body length, not including legs, given in millimetres.

Other invertebrates. Length of body, given in millimetres or centimetres.

Mammals. Length of head and body (H&B), not including tail, given in centimetres.

Birds. Length of bird from beak to tip of tail, given in centimetres.

Flowers, ferns, trees, mosses and **grasses**. Height from ground level to the top of the plant, given in centimetres or metres.

Spotting wildlife in cities

At first sight it may seem that there is no wildlife in a city — just concrete, tarmac, buildings, fumes, noise and traffic. But if you start to look around, you will find plenty of places where wild plants and animals can and do live.

All towns have churchyards, parks and derelict or waste places; many have canals and rivers where you can spot wildlife. Rubbish tips, factory yards, playing fields, railway sidings, old gravel pits and river-banks are all good places to look. Be careful when you go spotting that you do not trespass on private land and be aware of danger: don't go near derelict buildings, for example, unless you are sure they are safe.

Look closely on tombstones and on tree trunks. Look in untidy corners of parks and gardens as well as on the surface of cultivated soil. Look in cracks in pavements and on the tops of walls.

You will even be able to spot wildlife in and around buildings. Look in bathrooms, kitchens, cellars and sheds. Many animals that are active at night hide in these places during the day.

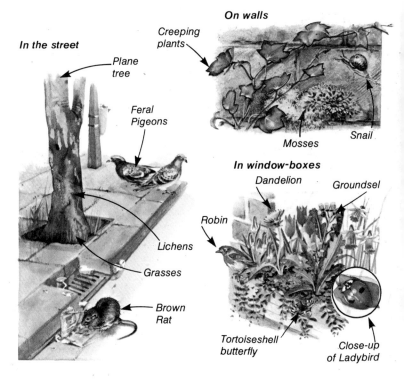

In the street
- Plane tree
- Feral Pigeons
- Lichens
- Grasses
- Brown Rat

On walls
- Creeping plants
- Mosses
- Snail

In window-boxes
- Dandelion
- Groundsel
- Robin
- Tortoiseshell butterfly
- Close-up of Ladybird

7

Dandelion ▶

Common weed with a rosette of leaves. The flowers close at night. Look for the "clock" of downy white fruits. Paths and waste places. 5-20 cm tall. March—Nov.

Dandelion "clock"

Flowers close at night

Fruiting head

Scales

◀ Coltsfoot

Flowers come out before the leaves. Look for woolly scales on flower stalks. Has a "clock" like the Dandelion. Bare ground and waste places. 5-30 cm tall. Feb.—April.

Large heart-shaped leaf

Tiny leaflets between larger ones

Silverweed ▶

Low plant with creeping stems. New plants are formed where stem roots. Paths, roadsides, damp and waste places. 10-20 cm tall. June—Aug.

Silvery underside to leaf

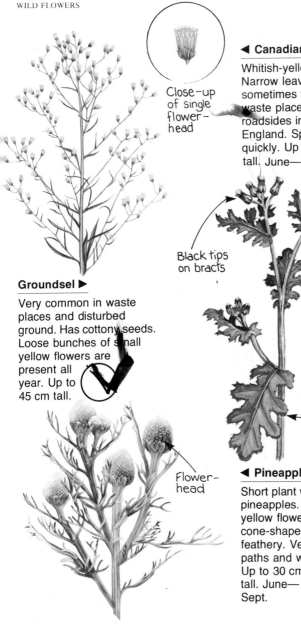

Close-up
of single
flower-
head

◀ Canadian Fleabane

Whitish-yellow flowers.
Narrow leaves are
sometimes toothed. Bare
waste places and
roadsides in southern
England. Spreads
quickly. Up to 1 m
tall. June—Oct.

Black tips
on bracts

Flowers
may be
nodding
or upright

Groundsel ▶

Very common in waste
places and disturbed
ground. Has cottony seeds.
Loose bunches of small
yellow flowers are
present all
year. Up to
45 cm tall.

Flower-
head

Leaves
have
wavy
edges

◀ Pineapple Weed

Short plant which smells of
pineapples. Greenish-
yellow flower-heads are
cone-shaped. Leaves are
feathery. Very common on
paths and waste places.
Up to 30 cm
tall. June—
Sept.

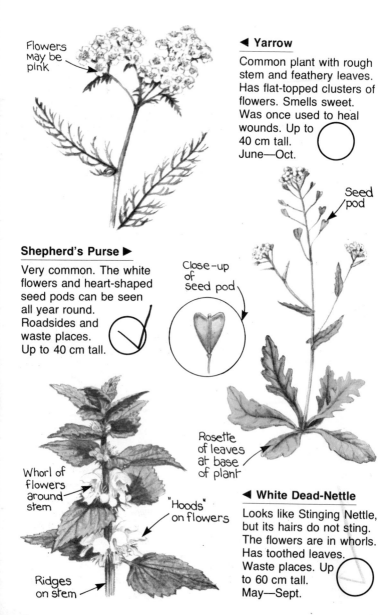

Flowers may be pink

◀ Yarrow

Common plant with rough stem and feathery leaves. Has flat-topped clusters of flowers. Smells sweet. Was once used to heal wounds. Up to 40 cm tall. June—Oct.

Seed pod

Shepherd's Purse ▶

Very common. The white flowers and heart-shaped seed pods can be seen all year round. Roadsides and waste places. Up to 40 cm tall.

Close-up of seed pod

Rosette of leaves at base of plant

Whorl of flowers around stem

"Hoods" on flowers

Ridges on stem

◀ White Dead-Nettle

Looks like Stinging Nettle, but its hairs do not sting. The flowers are in whorls. Has toothed leaves. Waste places. Up to 60 cm tall. May—Sept.

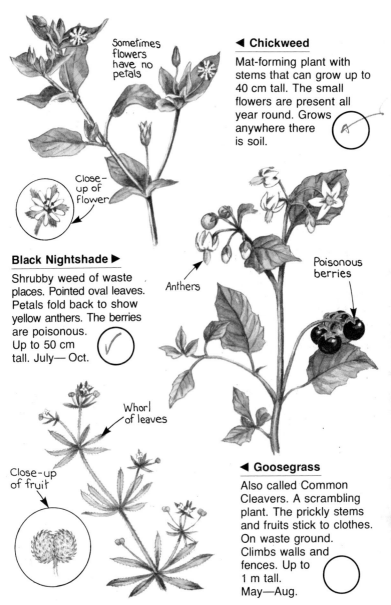

Sometimes flowers have no petals

◄ Chickweed

Mat-forming plant with stems that can grow up to 40 cm tall. The small flowers are present all year round. Grows anywhere there is soil.

Close-up of flower

Black Nightshade ►

Shrubby weed of waste places. Pointed oval leaves. Petals fold back to show yellow anthers. The berries are poisonous. Up to 50 cm tall. July— Oct.

Anthers

Poisonous berries

Whorl of leaves

Close-up of fruit

◄ Goosegrass

Also called Common Cleavers. A scrambling plant. The prickly stems and fruits stick to clothes. On waste ground. Climbs walls and fences. Up to 1 m tall. May—Aug.

9

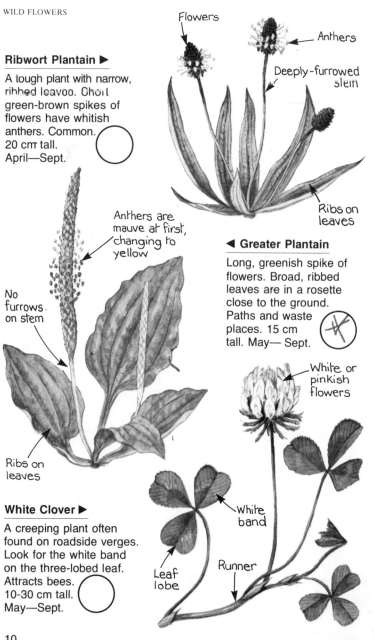

Ribwort Plantain ▶

A tough plant with narrow, ribbed leaves. Short green-brown spikes of flowers have whitish anthers. Common. 20 cm tall. April—Sept.

Flowers

Anthers

Deeply-furrowed stem

Ribs on leaves

Anthers are mauve at first, changing to yellow

No furrows on stem

Ribs on leaves

◀ Greater Plantain

Long, greenish spike of flowers. Broad, ribbed leaves are in a rosette close to the ground. Paths and waste places. 15 cm tall. May— Sept.

White or pinkish flowers

White Clover ▶

A creeping plant often found on roadside verges. Look for the white band on the three-lobed leaf. Attracts bees. 10-30 cm tall. May—Sept.

White band

Leaf lobe

Runner

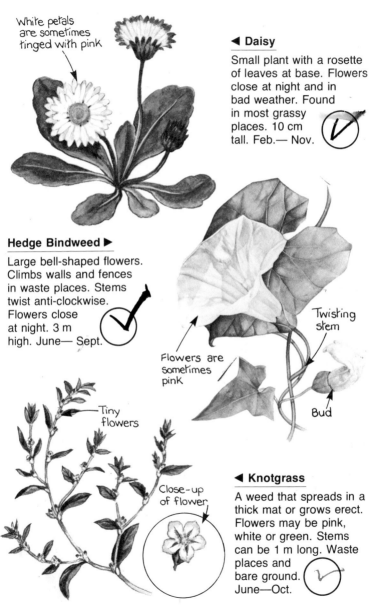

White petals are sometimes tinged with pink

◀ Daisy

Small plant with a rosette of leaves at base. Flowers close at night and in bad weather. Found in most grassy places. 10 cm tall. Feb.— Nov.

Hedge Bindweed ▶

Large bell-shaped flowers. Climbs walls and fences in waste places. Stems twist anti-clockwise. Flowers close at night. 3 m high. June— Sept.

Flowers are sometimes pink

Twisting stem

Bud

Tiny flowers

Close-up of flower

◀ Knotgrass

A weed that spreads in a thick mat or grows erect. Flowers may be pink, white or green. Stems can be 1 m long. Waste places and bare ground. June—Oct.

11

Notch in petal

Common Mallow ▶

Can be erect or sprawling.
Stem leaves have deep
lobes. Derelict places.
Attracts bees.
Stems up to
90 cm long.
June—Sept.

Buds

Seed with
hairy
"parachute"

◀ Rosebay Willowherb

Also called Fireweed. Tall,
erect plant with spikes
of pink flowers. Long,
narrow leaves. Common on
waste ground. Up
to 1 m tall.
July—Sept.

Hairy
seeds
are
inside
long
pods

Great Willowherb ▶

Also known as Codlins-
and-Cream. Has hairy
seeds. By canals, ponds
and damp places. About
1 m tall with
a hairy stem.
July—Aug.

Leaves
are
hairy

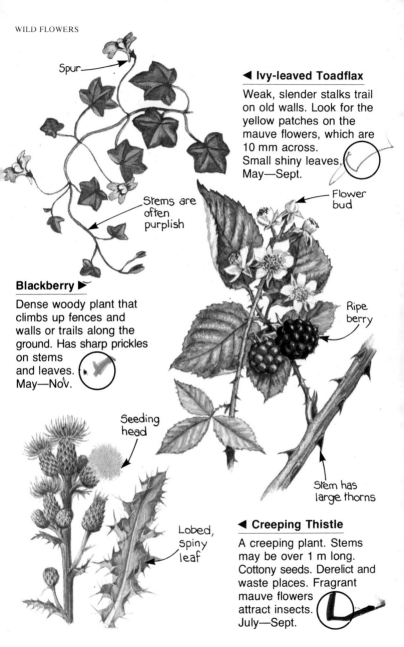

Spur

◀ Ivy-leaved Toadflax

Weak, slender stalks trail on old walls. Look for the yellow patches on the mauve flowers, which are 10 mm across. Small shiny leaves. May—Sept.

Stems are often purplish

Flower bud

Blackberry ▶

Dense woody plant that climbs up fences and walls or trails along the ground. Has sharp prickles on stems and leaves. May—Nov.

Ripe berry

Seeding head

Stem has large thorns

Lobed, spiny leaf

◀ Creeping Thistle

A creeping plant. Stems may be over 1 m long. Cottony seeds. Derelict and waste places. Fragrant mauve flowers attract insects. July—Sept.

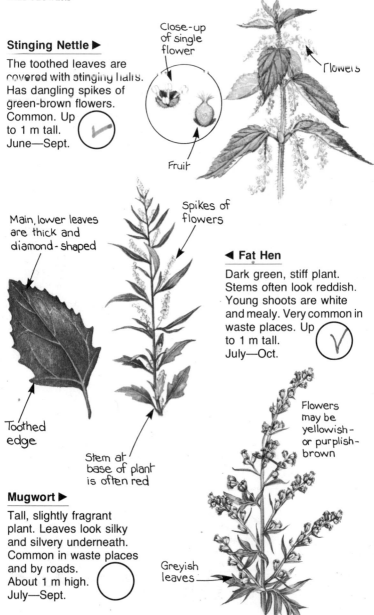

Stinging Nettle ▶

The toothed leaves are covered with stinging hairs. Has dangling spikes of green-brown flowers. Common. Up to 1 m tall. June—Sept.

Close-up of single flower

Flowers

Fruit

Spikes of flowers

Main, lower leaves are thick and diamond-shaped

◀ Fat Hen

Dark green, stiff plant. Stems often look reddish. Young shoots are white and mealy. Very common in waste places. Up to 1 m tall. July—Oct.

Toothed edge

Stem at base of plant is often red

Flowers may be yellowish- or purplish-brown

Mugwort ▶

Tall, slightly fragrant plant. Leaves look silky and silvery underneath. Common in waste places and by roads. About 1 m high. July—Sept.

Greyish leaves

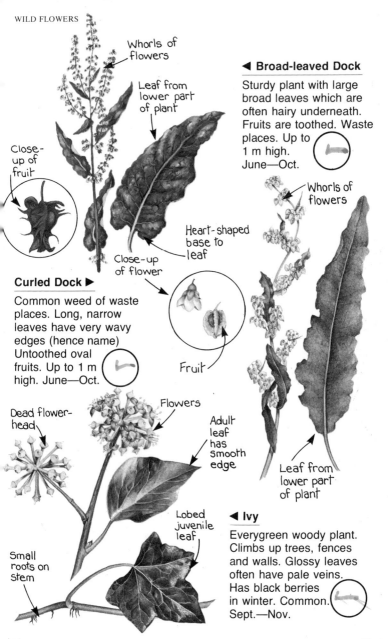

Whorls of flowers

Leaf from lower part of plant

Close-up of fruit

◀ Broad-leaved Dock

Sturdy plant with large broad leaves which are often hairy underneath. Fruits are toothed. Waste places. Up to 1 m high. June—Oct.

Whorls of flowers

Heart-shaped base to leaf

Close-up of flower

Curled Dock ▶

Common weed of waste places. Long, narrow leaves have very wavy edges (hence name) Untoothed oval fruits. Up to 1 m high. June—Oct.

Fruit

Dead flower-head

Flowers

Adult leaf has smooth edge

Leaf from lower part of plant

Lobed juvenile leaf

◀ Ivy

Everygreen woody plant. Climbs up trees, fences and walls. Glossy leaves often have pale veins. Has black berries in winter. Common. Sept.—Nov.

Small roots on stem

Very dark, green crown

Needles are parted on twig

▲ Yew

Dark green needles—new growth is lighter in colour. Red berry-like fruits are poisonous. Orange-brown flaking bark. Often planted in churchyards. Up to 25 m tall.

Poisonous berry

Long blunt bud

Short paired needles

▲ Scots Pine

Short, blue-green, paired needles. Upper bark is orangey, but grey and furrowed below. There are several varieties. 35 m tall.

Green cone ripens to brown in second year

Sparse-looking crown

▲ London Plane

Large broad leaves with pointed lobes. Spiny "bobble" fruits hang all winter. Flaking bark leaves yellowish patches. Planted in streets. 30 m tall.

Ripe fruit

Large lobed leaf has toothed edge

▲ Sycamore

Dark green, leathery leaves with five lobes. Paired, closely-angled, winged seeds. Smooth brown bark becoming scaly. 25-30 m tall.

Fruits twist as they fall

17

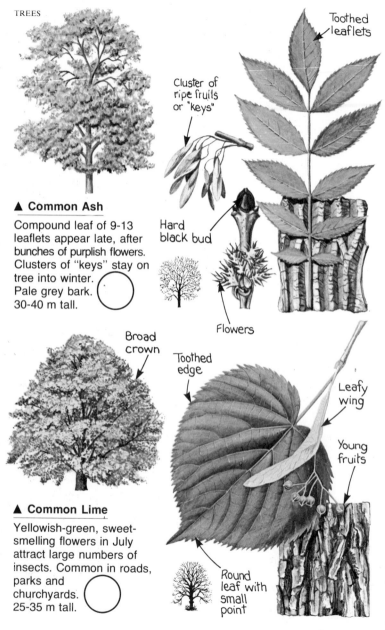

Toothed leaflets

Cluster of ripe fruits or "keys"

Hard black bud

Flowers

▲ Common Ash

Compound leaf of 9-13 leaflets appear late, after bunches of purplish flowers. Clusters of "keys" stay on tree into winter. Pale grey bark. 30-40 m tall.

Broad crown

Toothed edge

Leafy wing

Young fruits

▲ Common Lime

Yellowish-green, sweet-smelling flowers in July attract large numbers of insects. Common in roads, parks and churchyards. 25-35 m tall.

Round leaf with small point

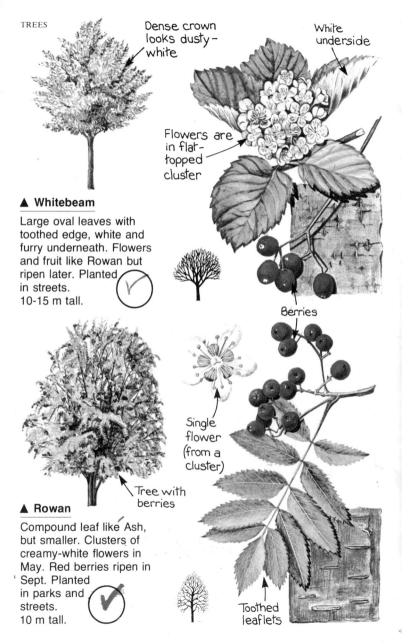

Dense crown looks dusty-white

White underside

Flowers are in flat-topped cluster

▲ Whitebeam

Large oval leaves with toothed edge, white and furry underneath. Flowers and fruit like Rowan but ripen later. Planted in streets.
10-15 m tall.

Berries

Single flower (from a cluster)

Tree with berries

▲ Rowan

Compound leaf like Ash, but smaller. Clusters of creamy-white flowers in May. Red berries ripen in Sept. Planted in parks and streets.
10 m tall.

Toothed leaflets

19

Tree in bloom

Leaves have 5-7 leaflets

Flowers

▲ Horse Chestnut

Compound leaf made up of 5-7 large leaflets. Upright "candle" of white (or pink) flowers in May. Parks and avenues. 25 m tall.

Conker (fruit) is in prickly case

Smooth-edged leaflet

▲False Acacia

Compound leaves of many small leaflets. Pairs of sharp thorns on twigs. Hanging clusters of white flowers in June. Deeply-furrowed bark.

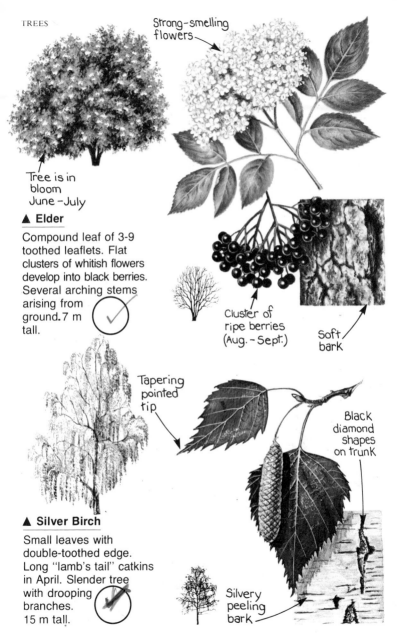

Strong-smelling flowers

Tree is in bloom June – July

▲ Elder

Compound leaf of 3-9 toothed leaflets. Flat clusters of whitish flowers develop into black berries. Several arching stems arising from ground. 7 m tall.

Cluster of ripe berries (Aug. – Sept.)

Soft bark

Tapering pointed tip

Black diamond shapes on trunk

▲ Silver Birch

Small leaves with double-toothed edge. Long "lamb's tail" catkins in April. Slender tree with drooping branches. 15 m tall.

Silvery peeling bark

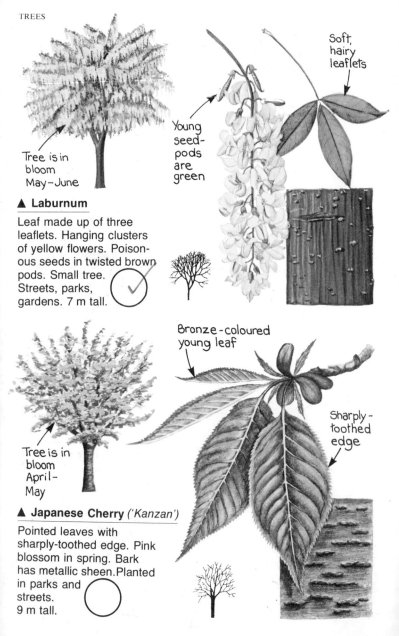

Tree is in bloom May–June

Soft, hairy leaflets

Young seed-pods are green

▲ Laburnum

Leaf made up of three leaflets. Hanging clusters of yellow flowers. Poisonous seeds in twisted brown pods. Small tree. Streets, parks, gardens. 7 m tall.

Bronze-coloured young leaf

Tree is in bloom April–May

Sharply-toothed edge

▲ Japanese Cherry ('Kanzan')

Pointed leaves with sharply-toothed edge. Pink blossom in spring. Bark has metallic sheen. Planted in parks and streets. 9 m tall.

Line of white streaks

White under tail

Red and yellow bill

Green legs

◀ Moorhen

Water bird that lives near ponds, lakes or canals. Flies only short distances. Eats seeds, insects, tadpoles, etc. Unafraid of people in parks. 33 cm.

Coot ▶

Found on lakes in town parks. Dives from water surface to feed on plants. Forms flocks in winter. Has large, lobed feet. 38 cm.

White bill and "forehead"

Female is dark brown

♀

Drooping crest

♂

◀ Tufted Duck

More common in winter. Often forms large groups. Feeds underwater on plants and animals. Can be seen on ponds in parks. 43 cm.

Distinctive white patch

Mallard ▶

Very common on town ponds, lakes and canals. Often "upends" but also feeds on water surface. Only the female "quacks" loudly. 58 cm.

♀

♂

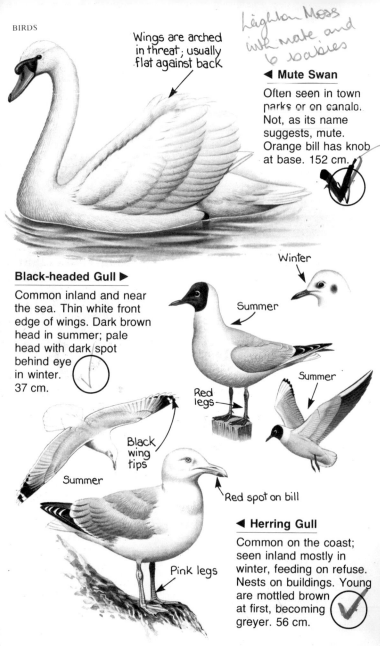

Wings are arched in threat; usually flat against back

Leighton Moss with mate and 6 babies

◀ Mute Swan

Often seen in town parks or on canals. Not, as its name suggests, mute. Orange bill has knob at base. 152 cm.

Black-headed Gull ▶

Common inland and near the sea. Thin white front edge of wings. Dark brown head in summer; pale head with dark spot behind eye in winter. 37 cm.

Winter

Summer

Red legs

Summer

Black wing tips

Summer

Red spot on bill

Pink legs

◀ Herring Gull

Common on the coast; seen inland mostly in winter, feeding on refuse. Nests on buildings. Young are mottled brown at first, becoming greyer. 56 cm.

Small round head

White on wings

Woodpigeon ▶

Common in town and city parks. Very tame in towns; often mixes with Feral Pigeons. Look for white patches on neck and wings. Forms large flocks in winter. 41 cm.

Often has white patches on wings

◀ Feral Pigeon

Domestic pigeons that have gone wild; descended from the wild Rock Dove, which nests on cliffs. Feral Pigeons nest on man-made cliffs—the ledges of buildings. Plumage varies. Very common. 33 cm.

Plumage can be blue, grey, brown white or chequered

Black half-collar on neck

Collared Dove ▶

Found in parks or large gardens. Eats seeds, berries, scraps. Nests in trees and on ledges. Sometimes seen in flocks. 30 cm.

Long white tail with black base

Swift ▶

A common migrant that visits Britain May—Aug. Flies fast over towns, in flocks, catching insects. Listen for its screaming call. 17 cm.

Forked tail is often closed to form a single point

Adult Swallow has tail with streamers

Long curved wings

White underparts

Red patch on throat and over bill

◀ Swallow

Summer migrant seen from April—Sept./Oct. Often feeds on insects over water. Builds nest on rafters or ledges in buildings. 19 cm.

Glossy blue back often looks black

House Martin has brilliant-white underparts

Broad white patch on rump

House Martin ▶

Summer migrant to Britain. Builds cup-shaped nest under eaves of houses and under bridges. Often in small colonies. Catches insects in flight. Look for its white rump. 13 cm.

Brownish wings

Juvenile

Starling ▶

Common even in the centre of large cities. In winter, the resident population in Britain is joined by millions of migrants from N. and E. Europe. 22 cm.

Adult in winter

Red breast and face

Short square tail

◀ Robin

Common in churchyards parks and gardens. Sings during winter and spring. Its alarm call is "tic-tic". Male and female look alike. 14 cm.

Song Thrush ▶

Found near or in trees or bushes. Well known for the way it breaks open snail shells. Also eats worms, insects and berries. Common in parks. 23 cm.

Dark brown plumage

♀

♂

◀ Blackbird

Lives where there are trees and bushes, often in parks or waste places. Some Blackbirds are part albino and have some white feathers. 25 cm.

Black plumage

Female is duller and browner than male

♂

◄ Chaffinch

Likely to be found wherever there are trees or bushes, including waste ground and parks. Often flocks with other finches in winter.
15 cm.

Silverdale ✓

Pink face and breast

♀

♂

Greenfinch ►

Found in similar places to Chaffinch. Likely to nest wherever there are trees and bushes. Eats weed seeds and berries.
15 cm.

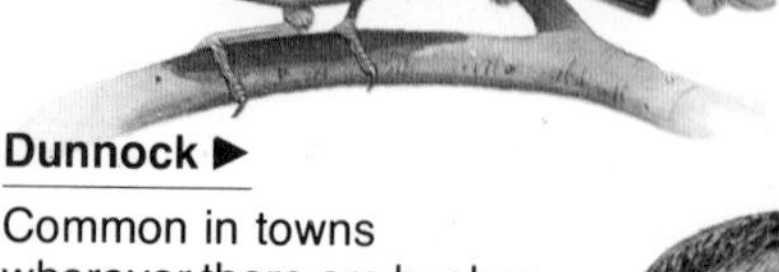

Silverdale

Bright yellow patches on wings and tail

♀

♂

◄ House Sparrow

Lives near houses and even in city centres, where it eats scraps, etc. Colour of birds in cities may be duller than shown here.
15 cm. ✓

Dunnock ►

Common in towns wherever there are bushes. Creeps about on ground looking for insects and seeds. Slate-grey face and breast.
14.5 cm. ✓

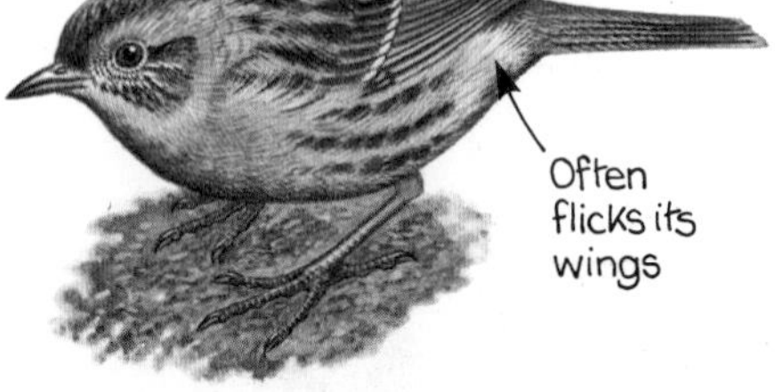

Often flicks its wings

Black Redstart ▶

Seen around derelict buildings, industrial sites and dumps, but rare in Britain. Nests on ledges of buildings. Eats insects. 14 cm.

♀

♂

Black face and breast

Red on tail

Blue cap

Narrow dark streak

Blue wings with white bar

◀ Blue Tit

Seen in parks, gardens and churchyards. Often raises its blue cap to form a small crest. Young are less colourful than adults. 11 cm.

Black head

Broad dark stripe

Great Tit ▶

Less numerous than Blue Tit, but seen in similar types of place. Nests in holes in trees. 14 cm.

Pied Wagtail

White Wagtail

◀ Pied/White Wagtail

White Wagtail is widespread in Europe, but in Britain we usually see only the Pied Wagtail. Common in towns. Feeds on insects. 18 cm.

29

Jackdaw ▶

Found in town parks or among old trees and buildings on outskirts of cities. Nests in colonies. 33 cm.

Grey on head

Blackish plumage has dull grey sheen

White eye

Black plumage

◀ Magpie

Increasingly common in cities. Eats insects and seeds and eggs from other birds' nests. Forms small flocks in winter. 46 cm.

Distinctive white belly

Hovers

♀

♂

Fan-shaped tail

Red-brown back with large black spots

Kestrel ▶

Well known for its hover when hunting, especially alongside roads. Often eats small birds in towns. May nest in buildings or trees in towns. 34 cm.

Long tail

Mole ▶

Lives underground.
Occasionally comes to
the surface. Molehills are
piles of waste earth from
its tunnels.
Not in
Ireland.
H&B 13 cm.

Strong
claws for
digging

Short
tail

Sharp prickles
on back

◀ Hedgehog

Mainly nocturnal. Rolls
into a ball when alarmed.
Eats animals like worms,
slugs and frogs. Snuffles,
squeals and snores.
Hibernates in compost
heaps, under
sheds, etc.
H&B 25 cm.

Hair underneath

Small
bat with
jerky
flight

Pipistrelle Bat ▶

Common in town parks
and squares. Flies after
sunset. Rests during the
day in hollow trees and
buildings. Eats flying
insects. Hibernates.
Wing span
20-30 cm.
BL 5 cm.

Roosting
bat

Soft
fur

Fur is usually brown
and rather
shaggy

Brown Rat ▶

In winter lives in buildings;
in summer moves to
sewers, canal and river
banks. Damages buildings.
Eats anything.
Max. H&B
26 cm.

Larger ears
than Brown
Rat

Sleek
fur

Shorter, fatter
tail than Black Rat's

Fur may be black or brown

◀ Black Rat

Rare: found only near
ports and coastal towns.
Lives in tops of buildings
such as warehouses.
Nocturnal. Climbs well.
Eats anything.
Max. H&B 20 cm.

Slender tail

House Mouse ▶

Grey variety lives in
buildings, while those in
bushes are browner. Eats
stored food and grain.
Mostly nocturnal. Infested
buildings
smell musty.
H&B 9 cm.

Long
pointed
muzzle

◀ Common Shrew

Found where there is
thick grass or bushes.
Not in Ireland. May nest
under rubbish. Fast-
moving. Eats
insects, worms.
H&B 7 cm.

Elephant Hawk ▶

Found on waste places,
even in city centres.
Eats Willowherb and
Fuchsia. Larva tapers at
head end like an
elephant's trunk.
Wing span 65 mm.

Head

♂

♀

Vapourer ◀

Common all over Britain.
Found anywhere in towns
where there are a few
trees. Female has only
wing stubs and
cannot fly.
Wing span 35 mm.

Hind wings
often look
pink

Cinnabar ▶

Often flies by day, but
weakly. Striped larvae
feed in groups on Ragwort.
Common on waste ground
and railway
banks. Wing span
40-45 mm.

Ragwort

Large Yellow Underwing ◀

Sometimes flies into houses
at night. Rests in Ivy on
walls during day. Larva
eats grasses and other
small plants. Common
everywhere.
Wing span
45-60 mm.

◀ Painted Lady

Arrives in spring from the Mediterranean. Adults cannot survive winter in Britain, but may fly south in autumn. Wing span 62-65 mm.

Lays eggs on thistles

Painted Lady

Red Admiral

Red Admiral ▶

Common in waste places on Buddleia and Michaelmas Daisies. Migrates here from the Mediterranean. Larvae feed on nettles. Wing span 66-68 mm.

Thistle

Small Tortoiseshell

Blue dots around wings

◀ Small Tortoiseshell

Name comes from pattern on wings, Visits many flowers and is common all over Britain. Has two broods. Larvae feed on nettles. On the wing April—Nov. Wing span 48-52 mm.

Small White ▶

Appears in April/May and
August. Lays single
eggs on cabbages and
Nasturtiums. Common in
waste places, parks
and gardens.
Wing span
48-50 mm.

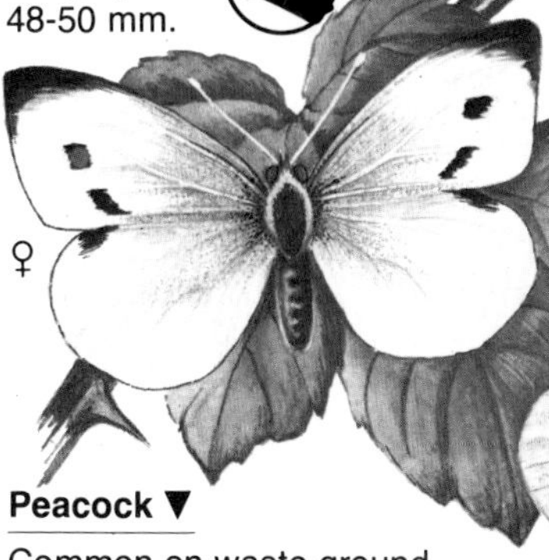

♂

♀

♀

♂

Peacock ▼

Common on waste ground.
Hibernates in adult stage,
in hollow trees, sheds, etc.
Lays eggs on nettles.
Larvae spin webs.
Wing span
62-68 mm.

Peacock

Markings
look like "eyes"
on a peacock's
tail

35

Actual size of insect

Common Wasp ▶

Ofton builds colonies in holes in the ground. Stings to kill prey. Often attracted by fruit or jam. Seen around dustbins. 11-20 mm long.

Two pairs of wings

◀ Leaf-cutter Bee

Cuts semi-circular pieces from rose leaves to make cylinders where the female lays a single egg provided with nectar and pollen. Solitary species. Male 10 mm long, female 11 mm.

Leaf cut by bee

Buff-tailed Bumblebee ▶

Very few survive the winter. Usually build nest for colony underground. 11-22 mm long.

One pair of wings

◀ Hoverfly

Looks like a small wasp but has only two wings. On sunny days, hovers then darts off quickly. Larvae eat aphids. Harmless. 11-14 mm long.

36

Very long legs

Common Cranefly ▶

Also called Daddy-long-legs. Sometimes flies into houses at night. Does not bite or sting. Larvae, called Leather-jackets, found in lawns. Adult is 17-25 mm long.

Grey and brown body

◀ Housefly

Very common. Attracted by food and rubbish. Can carry diseases. Larvae are legless maggots. 7-8 mm long.

Blowfly ▶

Also called Bluebottle. Makes loud buzzing sound. Lays eggs on dead animals or on meat left uncovered. Very common. Seen March—October. 9-15 mm long.

Blue hairy body

◀ Green Lacewing

Sometimes attracted to house lights. Often goes into houses and garden sheds to hibernate. Larvae eat aphids. 15 mm long.

Larva catching aphid

Common Froghopper ▶

Good at jumping. Nymph lives on plant juices, forming a froth ("cuckoo spit") on stems. Adult is 5-6 mm long.

Adult on blade of grass

Nymph is inside "spit"

Rose twig

◀ Greenfly

Green or pinkish. Often on roses in spring, then moves to other plants. Excretes honeydew which ants feed on. Is a pest on roses. 2-3 mm long.

Common Cockroach ▶

In houses and other warm buildings, where it eats waste. Females lay eggs in purse-like containers. Does not fly. Active at night. 25 mm long.

Bread

Bread

◀ German Cockroach

Now more common than Common Cockroach. Lives in restaurants, hospitals bakeries, etc. Hides during day in warm places. 13 mm long.

Ladybird
eating Greenfly

Two-spot Ladybird ▶

Very common. Colour
pattern often varies and
some individuals are
shiny black
with red spots.
4-5 mm long.

◀ Seven-spot Ladybird

Very common in parks and
on waste places. Spends
the winter in houses, sheds
or tree under bark. Emerges
on sunny spring days;
found throughout
summer
6-7 mm long.

Devil's Coach Horse ▶

When challenged, raises
tail and spreads jaws. Can
ooze poisonous liquid from
end of abdomen. Eats
insect larvae,
snails, slugs, etc.
25-30 mm long.

Adult

Larva

Adult

Larva

◀ Cockchafer

Generally scarce in towns.
Flies around tree-tops in
early summer and
sometimes strays
indoors. Larvae live
underground and
eat plant roots.
25-30 mm long.

39

Silverfish ▶

Wingless, silvery insect
that lives in bathrooms,
kitchens, etc. of old houses.
Active at night. Runs to
shelter when light
is turned on.
About 10 mm long.

Shiny,
silvery body

Runs
very quickly
on tiny legs

Forceps are
raised when
earwig is
threatened

♀   ♂

◀ Common Earwig

Eats small, usually dead
insects, as well as leaves,
fruits, etc. Female guards
larvae until they can
look after
themselves.
15 mm long.

Hind wings may be
missing (as here) –
the ♀ chews them
off during
mating

House Cricket ▶

Often found in new
buildings and on rubbish
tips. Makes a chirping
sound. Has large hind-legs
for jumping.
Harmless.
20 mm long.

♂

Winged
ants

Wingless
worker
ant

◀ Black Ant

Lives under paving stones
and rocks. May go into
houses in search of sweet
food. Winged male and
female ants swarm
in autumn.
3-9 mm long.

Garden Slug ▶

Most often seen after
rain, on summer nights,
on soil or wet paths.
Spends daytime in shady
damp places. Burrows to
feed on roots.
Waste places, parks,
etc. 25-30 mm long.

Leaves
yellow-orange
slime
trail

Thick black line
and groove on
side

Mottled with
darker
markings

Breathing
hole

◀ Netted Slug

Very common. Leaves
white slime on paths.
Eats fruit, leaves and
roots of plants.
A serious pest.
35 mm long.

Garden Snail ▶

Found everywhere, on
long grass or on old walls.
Hides under stones during
the day. Feeds on plants
at night.
Shell is
25-35 mm
across.

Large, thick
shell

Greyish body

Brownish-red
at front end

◀ Earthworm

Burrows in soil, eating
dead plant matter. Pulls
in leaves to plug up
the end of its burrow.
Often seen on
surface
after rain.
10-30 cm long.

Pale
back
end

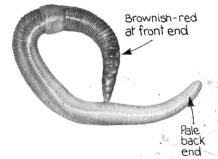

Woodlouse ▶

Oniscus asellus
Lives in damp places,
including cellars. May be
grey or yellowish with
paler patches.
Active at night.
15-18 mm long.

◀ Woodlouse

Porcellio scaber
Usually grey, sometimes
has black dots. Cellars,
under stones and bark.
Nocturnal.
Eats plants.
11-18 mm long.

Centipede ▶

Lives under stones or in
damp, dark places like
cellars. Sometimes seen
in baths. Can poison and kill
insects and slugs with
its front claws.
18-30 mm
long.

Legs are
lighter
brown than
body

Cylindrical
body

◀ Snake Millipede

Lives in soil, under
stones or in other dark
places. Eats plant roots.
Active at night. Sometimes
enters houses.
20-30 mm
long.

Has about 100
pairs of legs

Harvestman ▶

Very common in and around buildings. Hunts at night for insects, spiders, etc. Most common in autumn. Female lays eggs in the ground. Body 4-9 mm long.

Small, round body

Very long legs

Black and white markings on body

Short legs

◀ Zebra Spider

Does not spin a web but jumps to catch its prey. Often seen, on sunny days, hunting on walls. Markings are for camouflage. Body 4-7 mm long.

Garden Spider ▶

Spins a web to catch flies and other insects. Often hangs head-down in the middle of its web. Female is much larger than the male. Body 7-18 mm long.

White pattern on body

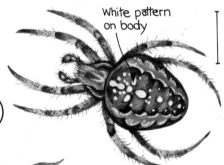

◀ House Spider

Large spider that lives in houses, sheds, etc. Often falls into baths. Spins a tangled web in odd corners. Common. Body 9-14 mm long.

Brown, hairy body

Small frond

Spore-producing structures

Wall Rue ▶

Dull green, leathery fronds have long stalks. Fronds grow in tufts from the underground stem. Grows on old limestone walls, particularly churches.
2-15 cm tall.

Underside of frond

Large frond

Kidney-shaped coverings hide spore-producing structures

◀ Male Fern

Common and widespread. Tops of walls, drains and other shady places. Has large fronds which usually die back in autumn.
40-100 cm tall.

Underside of frond

Fertile stem produces spores

Sections of branches break off easily

Field Horsetail ▶

Pinkish-brown fertile stems appear in spring. Larger, green shoots with whorls of branches appear later. Waste places.
10-90 cm tall.

Ridges on stem

Whorl of branches

44

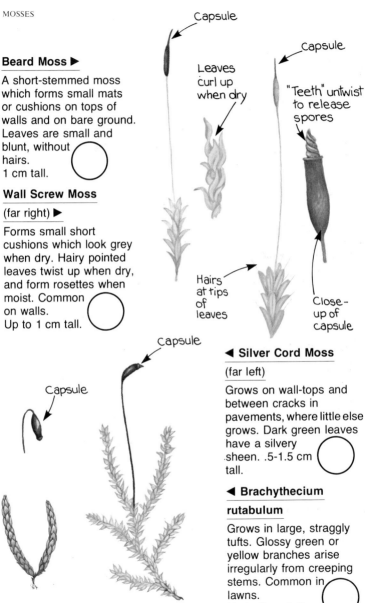

Beard Moss ▶

A short-stemmed moss which forms small mats or cushions on tops of walls and on bare ground. Leaves are small and blunt, without hairs.
1 cm tall.

Wall Screw Moss

(far right) ▶

Forms small short cushions which look grey when dry. Hairy pointed leaves twist up when dry, and form rosettes when moist. Common on walls.
Up to 1 cm tall.

Capsule

Leaves curl up when dry

Capsule

"Teeth" untwist to release spores

Hairs at tips of leaves

Close-up of capsule

Capsule

Capsule

◀ Silver Cord Moss

(far left)

Grows on wall-tops and between cracks in pavements, where little else grows. Dark green leaves have a silvery sheen. .5-1.5 cm tall.

◀ Brachythecium

rutabulum

Grows in large, straggly tufts. Glossy green or yellow branches arise irregularly from creeping stems. Common in lawns.
Up to 5 cm tall.

45

Do not taste any fungus without expert advice.

Common Ink Cap ▶

Gills, at first dirty white, turn brown then black. Cap dissolves with age. At base of broadleaved trees, in gardens and on bare ground. May—Dec. Cap 3-7 cm wide.

Ring-like zones at base of stem

Ribs

Rings of colour on cap

Pale edge

◀ Coriolus versicolor

Brightly coloured fungus with velvet-like cap. Grows in layers on cut stumps and branches of broadleaved trees. All year round. Cap 2-5 cm wide.

Section of underside of Coriolus versicolor

Small pores under cap

Coral Spot Fungus ▶

Grows on damp twigs and dead branches of trees. Groups of small pale pink dots turning dark red-brown. Common. All year round. 3-4 mm across.

Rotting log

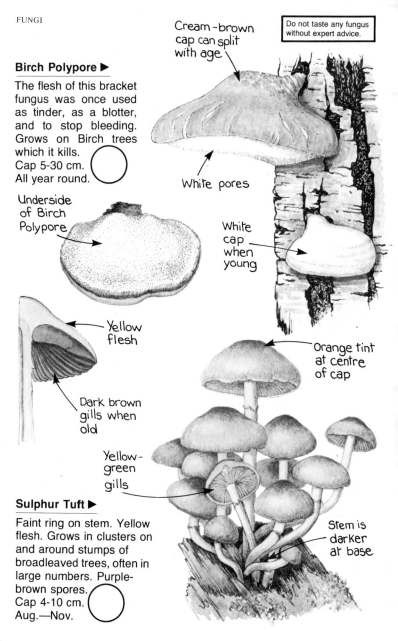

Do not taste any fungus without expert advice.

Cream-brown cap can split with age

Birch Polypore ▶

The flesh of this bracket fungus was once used as tinder, as a blotter, and to stop bleeding. Grows on Birch trees which it kills.
Cap 5-30 cm.
All year round.

White pores

Underside of Birch Polypore

White cap when young

Yellow flesh

Dark brown gills when old

Orange tint at centre of cap

Yellow-green gills

Sulphur Tuft ▶

Faint ring on stem. Yellow flesh. Grows in clusters on and around stumps of broadleaved trees, often in large numbers. Purple-brown spores.
Cap 4-10 cm.
Aug.—Nov.

Stem is darker at base

47

Fruiting
structures

◄ Common Orange Lichen

An easily-spotted dics-like lichen which forms patches on roofs, tombstones and walls of basic material. Patches about 15 cm across.

Forms a thick crust with a powdery surface

Grey Crust Lichen ►

The commonest crust lichen of town centres. It forms an inconspicuous thick crust with no clear edges. Found on walls, pavements, tombstones, trees.

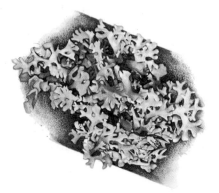

◄ Parmelia physodes

A leafy kind of lichen, common on fences, walls, trees or soil. It forms bluish-grey patches of narrow lobes with swollen ends. It is dark grey or black below.

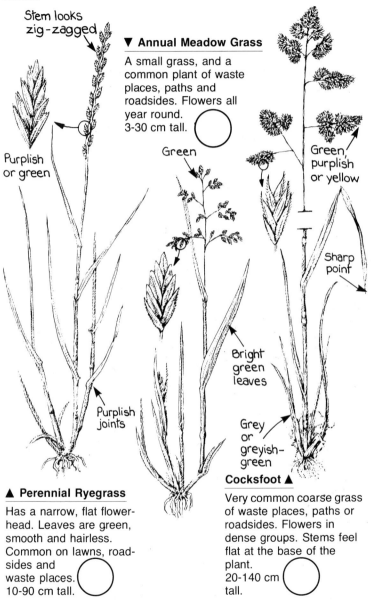

Stem looks zig-zagged

Purplish or green

▼ Annual Meadow Grass

A small grass, and a common plant of waste places, paths and roadsides. Flowers all year round. 3-30 cm tall.

Green

Green, purplish or yellow

Sharp point

Bright green leaves

Purplish joints

Grey or greyish-green

▲ Perennial Ryegrass

Has a narrow, flat flower-head. Leaves are green, smooth and hairless. Common on lawns, road-sides and waste places. 10-90 cm tall.

Cocksfoot ▲

Very common coarse grass of waste places, paths or roadsides. Flowers in dense groups. Stems feel flat at the base of the plant. 20-140 cm tall.

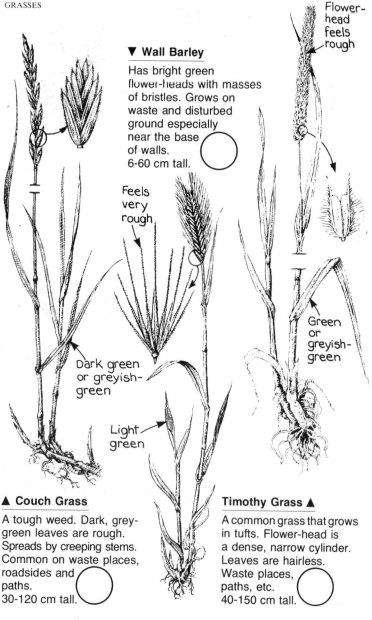

Flower-
head
feels
rough

▼ Wall Barley

Has bright green
flower-heads with masses
of bristles. Grows on
waste and disturbed
ground especially
near the base
of walls.
6-60 cm tall.

Feels
very
rough

Green
or
greyish-
green

Dark green
or greyish-
green

Light
green

▲ Couch Grass

A tough weed. Dark, grey-
green leaves are rough.
Spreads by creeping stems.
Common on waste places,
roadsides and
paths.
30-120 cm tall.

Timothy Grass ▲

A common grass that grows
in tufts. Flower-head is
a dense, narrow cylinder.
Leaves are hairless.
Waste places,
paths, etc.
40-150 cm tall.

Problems for wildlife

Living in a town presents problems for many plants and animals. All animals rely directly or indirectly on plants for food and shelter — but there are not many places for wild plants to grow in a town. There is little soil as most of the ground is covered with tarmac or concrete. Many lawns in parks and churchyards are weeded or sprayed with herbicides to kill wild plants.

Even if a plant can find a place to grow, it faces other difficulties. All plants need oxygen from the air to live. Green plants also need carbon dioxide and sunlight to make food (photosynthesis). Smoke and other air pollutants can block up the pores in a plant's leaves so that it cannot get oxygen or carbon dioxide from the air. Smog and dust also cut down the amount of sunlight that reaches the plant.

Chemicals which collect on the leaves of plants in polluted areas can kill insects that eat the leaves. If birds eat these insects, they too can be affected.

Some birds do not live in urban areas because there is nowhere suitable for them to nest or feed. Their natural habitat may be an area such as a moor, which is completely different from a town. Many mammals avoid towns as they are very secretive, and need a secluded place in which to breed.

Although some plants and animals will never live in towns or cities, others are well suited to urban life. Some animals, such as Starlings, rats and Feral Pigeons, take advantage of man's presence and congregate in vast numbers, often becoming a pest.

London Plane trees are well suited to town life. They regularly shed patches of bark — and with it all the soot and grime it has collected. Underneath is new, clean bark. Like all deciduous trees, they lose their old, dirty leaves every autumn and grow a new, fresh set each spring.

Feral Pigeons are also well suited to town life. They are unafraid of people and traffic, feeding on scraps of food left by man. They nest on ledges on buildings. (See also page 25).

Most **conifers** do not grow well in towns. Although they produce some new leaves each year they do not shed their entire foliage every autumn. Some needles stay on the tree for several years, and their pores get clogged with grime.

Adapting to urban life

Some animals are naturally suited to town life. Others have changed and adapted their behaviour or appearance to fit into urban areas.

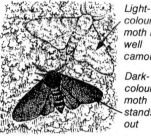

Light-coloured moth is well camouflaged

Dark-coloured moth stands out

▲ **Bark in unpolluted area**

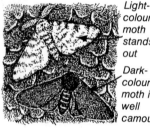

Light-coloured moth stands out

Dark-coloured moth is well camouflaged

▲ **Bark in polluted area**

◄ Peppered Moths

Peppered Moths have light-coloured wings, speckled with darker markings. During the day, they rest on the bark of trees. They are well camouflaged against the bark and lichens which are often widespread on tree trunks in unpolluted areas.

About 1850, after the industrial revolution, a dark form of Peppered Moth was noticed. It was found first in nothern industrial towns where smoke from factories had covered the lichens on the tree trunks with dark grey soot. The dark form had evolved and because it was well camouflaged against the dark tree trunks it was less likely to be seen and eaten by birds. Light-coloured moths were still found in the countryside, as were dark forms.

Now, after the Clean Air Acts, our cities are becoming cleaner and light-coloured moths are becoming more common.

House Martins ►

House Martins collect mud from the edges of ponds, streams and puddles to build their nests. They build cup-shaped nests, with a small entrance hole, under the eaves of houses. But where did they nest before people built houses?

In some areas their nests are found on cliffs and crags, under overhanging ledges. This is assumed to be their natural habitat. They have adapted so successfully to urban life that their nests are now very rare on cliffs but common on houses.

Mapping air pollution

Lichens are very sensitive to air pollution, and some kinds of lichens can grow in more polluted air than others. We can find out how polluted the air is by seeing which types of lichens are present.

Lichens have no roots, and so they rely on nutrients dissolved in rain-water. But when they absorb the rain, they also absorb any air pollutants that are dissolved in it, such as sulphur dioxide which is found in car exhaust and in smoke. Sulphur dioxide particles dissolve in rain making it slightly acid. In some polluted areas you may find lichens growing on walls, roofs or tombstones but not on trees. This is because the mortar, stone or asbestos is made of basic, alkaline, material, which reduces the effect of the acid rain.

Churchyard survey

To see how polluted your town is, do the following churchyard survey. Churchyards are good places to study lichens as there are plenty of places for them to grow and you do not need to ask permission to do your survey.

Choose several churchyards in different parts of your town: e.g. in the town centre; near a busy main road; near an industrial estate; on the edges of the town. You can plot the churchyards on a map to see where the most polluted parts of the town are.

At each churchyard, look for the types of lichens shown in the chart on this page. If you find, for example, leafy lichens growing on trees, this means the air is fairly unpolluted compared to an area where you find only powdery green alga. Even if you find other lichens such as disc or crusty lichens with the leafy lichens you can still mark the area on your map as being level 1, because in clean areas, many types of lichens will be able to grow.

Try to find out why some areas are more polluted than others; where is the pollution coming from and which way does the wind usually blow?

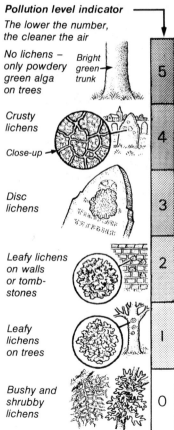

Pollution level indicator

The lower the number, the cleaner the air

No lichens – only powdery green alga on trees — Bright green trunk — **5**

Crusty lichens

Close-up — **4**

Disc lichens — **3**

Leafy lichens on walls or tombstones — **2**

Leafy lichens on trees — **1**

Bushy and shrubby lichens — **0**

Recent arrivals to towns

The ecology of our towns is always changing. You will be able to find some plants and animals in your town that your grandparents could not have seen in towns when they were young. Birds like the Feral Pigeon, and flowers like Groundsel, have been found in our towns for a long time, but some species have only recently invaded urban areas.

These plants and animals can be called "opportunists" — that is, they take advantage of an opportunity, such as a new place to live or a new source of food. Some of them, like the Fox, have moved into cities from the countryside. Others have arrived from abroad.

Oxford Ragwort ▶

Oxford Ragwort was first brought to this country over 200 years ago and was planted in the Oxford Botanic Gardens. It grows wild on the slopes of Mount Etna in Sicily. Like all the ragworts, this species has light, airborne seeds which are easily blown by the wind. Before long, Oxford Ragwort spread from the Botanic Gardens along railway lines where the rubble on the tracks was very like the volcanic cinders of Mount Etna; speeding trains carried along seeds in the air currents. Now Oxford Ragwort can be found on waste ground in towns and cities as far north as southern Scotland.

◀ Black Redstart

Before the 1920s the Black Redstart was a migrant which bred only very rarely in Britain, on cliffs. It was not until the 1940s that it began to breed regularly in this country. Buildings, bombed in the war, provided excellent nesting sites for the birds which fed on insects amongst the vegetated ruins. After the war, many of the bombed buildings were redeveloped, but the Black Redstart stayed. It now nests on power stations, gas works and other buildings. It is still a rare bird, most frequent in southern England, but it seems to be spreading to towns further and further north.

◀ Fox

Most Foxes live in the countryside, making their dens in woods, and eating rabbits, worms, etc. But recently more foxes have ventured into cities in search of food. You might catch a glimpse of one as it stealthily looks for food at night, or you might hear its barking call. Foxes live on railway embankments and scavenge food from rubbish tips, dustbins, and bird-tables.

Buddleia ▶

Buddleia was introduced to this country from China about 85 years ago and was widely planted in gardens. It spreads by tiny, winged seeds and became very common on bombed sites after the second world war. It can now be found on most waste places in southern England. In summer its spikes of strongly-scented lilac flowers attract many butterflies and other insects.

◀ Collared Dove

Collared Doves have only colonised Britain in the last 25 years. They spread across Europe from Asia, making use of man-made objects like pylons and cables to perch on and feed from. Now they are common residents, nesting in trees and on buildings on the outskirts of towns and cities. They eat grain and are especially plentiful in docks where grain is often spilt.

Animals and plants may be called "opportunists" without being a new arrival to an area. Blue Tits and Great Tits show an interesting example of opportunism in their habit of pecking through milk bottle tops to get at the cream.

Colonising waste places

There are derelict or waste places in every town. They are often next to car parks, near factories or by railway stations. Sometimes waste places are left when old houses or factories are knocked down and nobody uses the land for building. These newly-derelict places are bare except for rubble and other debris, but it is not long before wildlife appears. The first plants to begin to grow in, or "colonise", bare ground and rubble are mosses, lichens and ferns whose tiny spores are blown in by the wind. The spores get lodged in cracks and crevices in walls and on the ground, and soon develop into new plants. Many of these plants can live entirely on nutrients dissolved in rain-water.

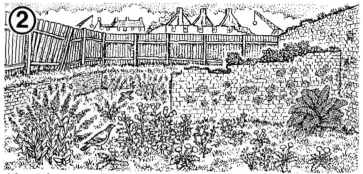

After a few years, more plants join the early colonisers on the waste ground. These are weeds, like Rosebay Willowherb, Dandelion and thistles. They all have light seeds which are easily carried by the wind. These plants grow best on bare ground where there is plenty of light and there are no other plants to crowd them out. Insects fly in to the waste place to feed on the flowers and lay their eggs. Pigeons, Sparrows and other similarly "bold" birds visit the area to eat insects and weed seeds, and may bring in tiny seeds or insects on their bodies.

Five years later there are even more plants growing on the waste ground. Plants like Goosegrass and Burdock have grown from barbed seeds which are carried in on people's clothes or on animals' fur. Apple trees may start to grow from cores thrown down by people crossing the site. Plants with berries, like Elder and Ivy, often grow from seeds dropped by birds after they have eaten the berries in other areas. The greater the variety of plants on the waste ground, the greater the variety of insects and birds that can feed and shelter there.

After 15 or 20 years the rubble and bare ground is hidden by climbing and scrambling plants. Bushes and trees have grown up and have crowded out many of the smaller weeds, which are unable to compete. Plants and flowers are visited by insects. Birds nest in the bushes and trees, and small animals, such as mice and shrews, find shelter amongst the long grass. The bare, derelict site is now teeming with wildlife.

This process — where bare ground is colonised by plants and animals, and eventually becomes covered with trees and bushes — is called "succession". Look for examples of the different stages in your town.

Glossary

Abdomen - the hind section of an insect.

Albino - a bird or mammal with white feathers or fur.

Anther - the part of a flower which produces the pollen.

Aphid - a type of insect, such as greenfly or blackfly.

Basic - the opposite of acidic; alkaline.

Bracket fungus - a flat-topped fungus which grows on trees and logs, and is shaped like a bracket.

Camouflage - the colouring or pattern on an animal that allows it to blend into its background, so that it is difficult to see.

Catkin - a hanging cluster of tiny flowers, found on some trees.

Colony - a group of plants or animals living together.

Colonise - the process by which plants and animals move into new areas.

Compound leaf - a leaf which is made up of several small leaflets.

Frond - the leaf-like part of a fern.

Gills (of fungi) - the ribs on the underside of some fungi, which radiate out from the stem like the spokes of a wheel.

Hibernation - when some animals spend the winter in an inactive state with a lower body temperature than usual, allowing them to survive without eating.

Honeydew - the sweet liquid excreted by some insects and eaten by others.

Invertebrates - animals without backbones, e.g. insects and worms.

Larva (plural: **larvae**) - the form which some insects and other animals take before they become adult, e.g. caterpillars of moths and butterflies.

Leaflet - a small leaf that forms part of a compound leaf.

Limestone - a type of rock often made up of the remains of sea creatures.

Migrant - an animal which regularly travels to another area or country.

Native (to Britain) - a species of plant or animal that has not been introduced by man.

Nocturnal - active mostly at night.

Nutrients (of plants) - substances, found in rain-water or in the soil, which are used by plants in order to grow.

Photosynthesis - the process by which the leaves and other green parts of a plant make food for the plant, using carbon dioxide from the air, water from the soil, and energy from sunlight.

Pollutant - a substance, such as a chemical waste, that causes pollution.

Rosette - a ring of leaves, usually growing very close to the ground surface, around the stem of a plant.

Runner (of a plant) - a stem which creeps over the surface of the ground, rooting at intervals and producing a new plant.

Spores - the minute reproductive cells of plants which do not produce seeds, such as mosses, ferns, fungi and lichens: often produced in thousands or millions.

Whorl - a ring of three or more leaves or flowers around the stem of a plant.

Books to read

Birds in Towns. Francesca Greenoak (Black's picture information books).
Birds of Towns. Neil Ardley (Almark).
The Ecology of Towns. Alfred Leutscher (Watts).
The Hidden Country. John Richards (Carousel).
The Natural History of Britain: Towns and Gardens. Denis Owen (Hodder & Stoughton).
The Pollution Handbook. Richard Mabey (Penguin).
The Unofficial Countryside. Richard Mabey (Sphere).
Wild Flowers of Verges and Waste Land. Jean Imrie (Black's picture information books).
Wild Life areas for schools. Durham County Conservation Trust (Durham).
Wild Life Begins at Home. Tony Soper (Pan).
Wild Life in House and Home. H. Mourier and O. Winding (Collins).

Useful addresses

If you write for information to any of the organisations listed here, please remember to enclose a **stamped, self-addressed envelope** for your reply.

The Nature Conservancy Council publishes wallcharts, posters, and books on urban wildlife and conservation. Their catalogue is available free from: Interpretative Branch, Nature Conservancy Council, Attingham Park, Shrewsbury SY4 4TW. Your envelope should be at least 20 cm x 21 cm.

Friends of the Earth run many local groups, some of which have sections for young people. Students and schoolchildren may join FOE for a reduced subscription, and take part in local or national activities concerned with conservation. For further information and the address of your local group, write to: Friends of the Earth, 9 Poland Street, London W1.

The British Trust for Conservation Volunteers, 10-14 Duke Street, Reading, Berks, organises practical conservation work for people over 16 years old.

The Royal Society for the Protection of Birds, The Lodge, Sandy, Beds, is the national society for anyone interested in birds. **The Young Ornithologists' Club** (Y.O.C.) is the junior section for people 15 years old and under.

You can get the address of your local **County Naturalists' Trust** from the Royal Society for Nature Conservation, 22 The Green, Nettleham, Lincoln LN2 2NR. They will also give you information about the WATCH club — the junior branch of the Nature Conservation Trusts. WATCH has its own magazine, special projects and local groups in all areas.

You can get the address of your local **Natural History Society** from CoEnCo, Zoological Gardens, Regents Park, London NW1.

Scorecard

The plants and animals in this scorecard are arranged in alphabetical order. When you go out spotting, fill in the date at the top of the blank columns, and then write in that column your score, next to each species that you see. At the end of the day, add up your score and put the total at the bottom of the column. Then add up your grand total.

	Score	Date	Date	Date		Score	Date	Date	Date
Acacia, False	10				Cockchafer	25			
Admiral, Red	15				Cockroach, Common	10			
Ant, Black	5				Cockroach, German	15			
Ash, Common	5				Cocksfoot	5			
Bat, Pipistrelle	20				Coltsfoot	5			
Barley, Wall	5				Coot	10			
Bee, Leaf-cutter	15				Coriolus versicolor	10			
Beetle, Devil's Coach Horse	10				Cranefly, Common	5			
Bindweed, Hedge	5				Cricket, House	20			
Birch, Silver	5				Daisy	5			
Blackbird	5				Dandelion	5			
Blackberry	5				Dead-Nettle, White	5			
Blowfly	5				Dock, Broad-leaved	5			
Brachythecium rutabulum	5				Dock, Curled	5			
Bumblebee, Buff-tailed	5				Dove, Collared	10			
Centipede	5				Duck, Tufted	10			
Chaffinch	5				Dunnock	5			
Cherry, Japanese	5				Earthworm	5			
Chestnut, Horse	5				Earwig, Common	5			
Chickweed	5				Elder	5			
Cinnabar Moth	15				Fat Hen	5			
Clover, White	5				Fern, Male	15			
Total					Total				

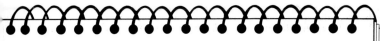

	Score	Date	Date	Date		Score	Date	Date	Date
Fleabane, Canadian	15				Lacewing, Green	10			
Grass, Couch	5				Ladybird, Seven-spot	5			
Grass, Timothy	10				Ladybird, Two-spot	5			
Greenfinch	10				Lichen, Common Orange	15			
Greenfly	5				Lichen, Grey Crust	5			
Groundsel	5				Lime, Common	10			
Gull, Black-headed	5				Magpie	10			
Gull, Herring	10				Mallard	5			
Harvestman	10				Mallow, Common	5			
Hawk Moth, Elephant	25				Martin, House	10			
Hedgehog	10				Millipede, Snake	10			
Horsetail, Field	20				Mole	25			
Housefly	5				Moorhen	10			
Hoverfly	5				Moss, Beard	10			
Ink Cap, Common	15				Moss, Silver Cord	5			
Ivy	5				Moss, Wall Screw	5			
Jackdaw	10				Mouse, House	10			
Kestrel	10				Mugwort	5			
Knotgrass	5				Nettle, Stinging	5			
Laburnum	5				Nightshade, Black	15			
Froghopper, Common	10				Painted Lady	15			
Fungus, Coral Spot	5				*Parmelia physodes*	10			
Goosegrass	5				Peacock (butterfly)	10			
Grass, Annual Meadow	5				Pigeon, Feral	5	17/8/86		
Total					Total				

	Score	Date	Date	Date		Score	Date	Date	Date
Pine, Scots	10				Starling	5			
Pineapple Weed	5				Sulphur Tuft	10			
Plane, London	5				Swallow	15			
Plantain, Greater	5				Swan, Mute	10			
Plantain, Ribwort	10				Swift	10			
Polypore, Birch	10				Sycamore	5			
Rat, Black	25				Thistle, Creeping	5			
Rat, Brown	5				Thrush, Song	5			
Redstart, Black	25				Tit, Blue	5			
Robin	5				Tit, Great	5			
Rowan	5	MD		↑	Toadflax, Ivy-leaved	10			
Rue, Wall	20				Tortoiseshell, Small	5			
Ryegrass, Perennial	5				Vapourer Moth	10			
Shepherd's Purse	5				Wagtail, Pied	10			
Shrew, Common	15				Wagtail, White	20			
Silverfish	10				Wasp, Common	5			
Silverweed	15				White, Small	5			
Slug, Garden	5				Whitebeam	10			
Slug, Netted	10				Willowherb, Great	10			
Snail, Garden	5				Willowherb, Rosebay	5			
Sparrow, House	5				Woodlouse (Oniscus asellus)	5			
Spider, Garden	5				Woodlouse (Porcellio scaber)	10			
Spider, House	5				Woddpigeon	5			
Spider, Zebra	15				Yarrow	5			
Total					Total				

	Score	Date	Date	Date		Score	Date	Date	Date
Yellow Under-wing, Large	10				Yew	10			
Total					Total			
					Grand Total			

Index

All scientific names are written in *italics*